OF WISDOM
AND WAR

Dear Leslie ~
Thank you for
Shining your light!
Jen

Jennifer Goodine

Of Wisdom and War
First edition 2022

www.wisewarrioryoga.com
wisewarrioryoga@gmail.com

ISBN: 979-8-218-11376-6

Cover design & illustration:
Esther Rai

Here's to all the warriors unafraid of finding the light within the darkness.
To all of us willing to feel pain so we may be free.

For Sophia and Liam,
the wisest warriors I have ever known

Words give a certain proof to your life.

Feelings, memories, moments, pain, and joy are all living inside waiting to be freed. I have spent my lifetime deeply mired in the words of others. Within their books, stories, songs, and cries I have searched for pieces of myself. Wandering through the metaphors I searched for validation of my own existence.

I never quite satiated that deep desire for certainty, always looking on the outside, to others. Rather, I was being invited to look inside of myself. As I learned to welcome stillness, I began to see my own light. I noticed that everything I had been searching for was already right inside of me. There is truth to the saying that sometimes what you seek is seeking you.

It was a seeking that led to a remembering, and that is how these words were born. These words yearned to emerge. To leave their mark upon these pages. Stories and moments, I hope, leave spaces for you to explore all that is seeking you too.

Contents

Part One

War

In the quest for love, truth and honor sacrifice will be made.
The warrior will rise from the deepest hole of despair and
look fear straight in the eyes and whisper,
"I am not afraid of the dark."

STRUGGLE

There's a tugging at my heart
Strings that aren't meant to cross
A mess of beautiful colors
The bleeding and blending of love and loss

.

A warrior's heart is her greatest weapon
and her only defense

The love between us lies
Like coals in the fire
Stubborn to die
But no longer aflame
Dull warmth
Still, we crave
This heat, waning
Yet familiar
A home for icy souls
Who melt at first touch
Remembering to reach
Not retract
From the friction of love
Dangerous
But all we have ever known

If my silence could scream
Above the waves
That wash your ears of knowing
All the sounds that let you see
How my heart breaks
When you believe
You already know what I need
Never curious
What fills my soul
Or what causes my spirit to bleed
The promise of true love
Barely survives
The thief of false belief

I dreamed myself awake
To the brightest lights I have ever seen
And my eyes knew exactly what to do
Wide open
Just as your arms
Waiting for me
And I may never sleep again
For fear of what I might miss
The patient rainbow
Rain
So pure, it gleams
A mountain's majesty
Just out of reach
Your love
It's reflection
In everything I see

What is the color of pain
Your heart blind to mine

You were gone before you left
The goodbye girl
Always sneaking out the back door
I never did understand
Your aversion to roots
Or why tiny spirits
Seemed to weigh you down
I tried to roam like you
But I was meant to tether
To matter much more sturdy
My lips
Longed to say hello

There is water
And there is fire
I bleed them both
Like rain storming from my eyes
When your desert heart is near
Like wind swirling in my throat
When your storms
Wash ashore
I am elemental
In your world
Accidental

My heart has hungered
For yours to bleed
Proof
That the dream is real
And this fractured fiction
Is just the story we tell
When we are too weary
To believe
Wake up to love, I beg
There is nothing to fear
When you become sovereign
Allowing
All that is true
To break through and breathe

There is noise
Hidden inside sorrow
Pleading for mercy
Behind silent
Eyes
Those that look right through
For fear of what they might see
A reflection denied
The shadow of the self
They are too afraid to greet

If you won't feel the war on the inside
You will fail to understand
What wars on the outside

Through rage
Flows a river
Ever changing
Rocks that own stories
And pave the way home
Containing the fires blazing
The only way to warm
These naked shores

I can hide behind the cloak of poetry
But the truth festers bare in my bones

All my heroes have hearts
Beautiful, by design
Even though the villain
Lives inside
So, what then is love
But a willingness to hold
Both the darkness and the shine
Within the whole of the sky

You cannot kill the monster
Without saying its name
Loud and crystal clear
Your resolute voice
The one weapon
It could possibly fear

I am hypnotized
By what is bright
All that your midnight
Cannot hide

The air had shackles
I couldn't see
A one hundred percent chance of humidity
And no storm in sight
Clouds heavy with ache
And I am barefoot
Waiting for rain
For some kind of break
Amnesty I deserve
Shelter I could take
But here I stand
Imprisoned by belief
Desperate for a cure
To be within your atmosphere
Such dangerous relief

Sincerity is born
Of a place that is still
Upon my heart
Yours casts a shadow
Of the deepest chill
This soul could withstand
When our lips part
Igniting a hunger
And all I taste is
Wasted wonder

I wrote a revolution in the sky
Laced with tears
Pieces of your lies
Leaving scribbles beneath the moon
Cryptic notes
Like puzzles to be solved
But you just see stars
When you open your eyes
Heavenly foreign bodies
Ephemeral and far away
While I claim the clouds
Melancholic and gray
For honesty belongs
And above you and surrounding
It shall stay

Promise dripped from her lips
Like autumn leaves
Pregnant with color
Desperate for release
And the earth collected
What your ears would not accept
Proof of life
The many circumstances
Of a daily death
What love embodies
All that is good and bad
That which cannot be classified
A heart bereft

These thoughts must go somewhere
They've already stained my heart
And I cannot decide
What should stay or what should go
So here I leave them
Before a page
Where soon all will know
The depths of my being
The fog over my chest
What sustains my soul
That which was pillaged
And the many pieces
Your entitled hands
Fumbled and left

The sheer force of you
I am frozen still
These naive waters
Never warmed to the chill
So I became what you never could
The keeper of dreams
She who holds space
The ever-present lighthouse
For all who are lost
And when the light fell upon me
I became the whole of the sea
The only trespass
You never dared to cross

Don't look for the clearing

Remember

You are the sword

You want to save her
But refuse to watch her bleed
Will not ask of her heart
Withholding the peace she needs
But it's warmth you want
Sharing only with her sides
Those you choose to see
And what's behind her eyes
When dusk arrives
Fueling the fire
Keeping love alive
So welcome the waiting
This gentle kindling
Passionate heat
Unhesitating

Jennifer Goodine

I have only ever wanted to be beholden
Not naked and exposed
Simply translucent
Promise emboldened
Yet it takes time to see
What is hidden behind these veils
For there is magic in the making
And my hands hold the key
To the treasures of the truth
My heart will not forsake

SURVIVE

You see madness, I find brave
Chasing fires through lightning storms
I'm mesmerized by a heart misbehaved

This disappointment
What breaks your heart
Spares your soul

She saw her mistakes like magic
She let wonder into her worry
And like the seasons
Ever-changing
The colors flooded her eyes
Releasing like the crimson leaves
Gracing the ground
Her feet, relieved
No longer in a rush
Nature is not meant to hurry

Sometimes you won't know
And this will require faith
To soften around the urge to run
To curiously listen
Until the crying is done
Put down your weapons
Remove the shield
A civil war is brewing
To conquer you must yield
To save love
To rescue a heart
Becoming peace is the path
The bravest warrior must chart

I have broken a thousand times
Come undone and cried
And waited alone
To see the sun rise
Never forgetting the sky
She becomes
A new day blooms to life
And I pick up the specks and shards
Revealing my wounds
Releasing the knife
Reverently announcing
All the many deaths
From which I have resurrected
Renewed
With newborn breath

There is a gift in destruction
From broken glass to war
Shiny little pieces scattered
Foreign unrest at your door
All of it a promise
Cautionary tales
To take to heart
Noticing how life is greater
Then the sum of its parts
So, when your whole falls to fragments
Please remember
Every beginning's end
Are the exact coordinates
Where hope arrives again

Some days are for breaking
Others you must steep
In a rush of tears
Through sweat and heat
Anointed with baptismal breath
For where you come apart
Is where you must rest
And where you stay
Fortifies the roots
Springtime awakens
As the sleepy flowers bloom

I will dust off this day
After I burn it to embers
Just a little sorceress
Who must welcome the heat
So she might always remember

Maybe I invited this hurricane
Romanced the clouds to attention
Woke destruction
Just to be mesmerized by the mess
See what happens
When the wild
Owns the wind

Light juxtaposes
What is desperate and bleak
Because love lingers
An invitation to reach
Beyond whatever you can see
The only way to rise
Is to take that brazen leap
How else might the raven
Find its wings

You are not exposed
You are unbound by belief
Undammed and wild
Mysterious as the sea

You left
And the breeze that followed
Fanned wanderlust
In these dusty wings
And I realized
Exodus is arrival
And home is everywhere
I choose to be

Jennifer Goodine

There are many words I have not told
These flavors of my mind
Exotic and bold
Both savory and sweet
I shall let them unfold
When I find your palate has expanded
And can withstand
The spicy heat I deliver
And the full experience I demand

42

I set myself on fire
Just to feel the burn
Anything to brighten the night sky
A gentle reminder for mother moon
In case her stars forget to shine

Remember who you are
When the world grows dim
There is a radiance desperate
To shine upon them
The pieces you have lost
Were never meant to stay
You have always been
The one to save the day
Both whole and secure
The savior you needed
When love was missing
And the path was obscured

Ah, to be drunk on promise
Coming to life in the spring
Knowing the frost will die
And the earth can hold
What you root
Will always rise

Let me run
Arms unfurled
Hair wild
Unencumbered as the wind
Don't wonder where I am headed
Or from where I have been
You might never witness
Such brilliance
Claim the sky with authority
Or this feral genius again

From a solid ground
You can reach
With an open heart
You will fly

My freedom calls
For you to sing
In unison with me
And each bird that spreads its wings
Gifts grace and liberty
The only way to survive
These tempestuous skies
What chaos calamity brings

If your heart can hold lifetimes
Why must you spend your days
Shallow in sorrow

They will tell you not to be soft
Exhale anyway
They will say you should shut your mouth
Breathe anyway
They will try to contort you
Within a tightly cornered box
Expand anyway
They might beat you, as winners often do
Fall down anyway
Who doesn't love to see the phoenix rise?

Where might you go
If only you could breathe
Would you stay settled
Benevolent as the oak tree
Or might you soar
Beyond the tips of the leaves
Up high without direction
As the crow flies through the breeze
What is it that brings that feeling of home
The familiar warmth of my love
Or the seduction of the unknown

I made art
Because I couldn't stand
On my feet
Before the world
Muddled in the crowd
I'd rather describe
Colors as feelings
And the sorrow that you hide
Because there is beauty in the ache
That is allowed to heal
Just by taking in
The pain others brave
Yet struggle to feel

There is a wild in the air
Breath like fire
Love amplified
An invitation to chase desire
Wind rushing at our backs
Fevered to attention
This life, a feast
Our starving hearts must devour
Such a beautiful mess
This wonderous heat
Combustible between us
Tiny little sparks
Of undeniable power

What dust have you let settle
Crack open your heart
Let your spirits breathe

How do you know when it's the right way
When your heart whispers louder
Then your mind screams
When you decide to stop running
Just to sit.
Just to stay

If only you could wait it out
After the rain has fallen
Once the sky cries in release
There is a clearing calling
The promise of peace
Let the horizon anoint your eyes
Set before you
Home that heals
Hope rises east

I am waiting for change
Like I am waiting on the rain
Desperate for a cleansing
Cautiously stripped
Just to feel alive
On my bare toes
Anticipating

Faith blooms
Wherever you seed love

Before you let your heart wither

Remember

You are the storm

The cleansing

The clearing

A lush oasis

The desert

Where desire is born

I became what you could not
Untangled these generational knots
For I am a mother of sun and earth
And this light that emanates
From the fractures of my heart
Has given the death of yours
Spontaneous rebirth

Part Two
Wisdom

When the mind rests, the body can feel.
This is when the soul speaks.

SURRENDER

It is not so much a letting go
Rather a welcoming
Like waves before the steady shore
The heart must rise and flow

If you only face the familiar
You will never hear
The symphony of summer's rain
Nor will you notice the shades of gray
December brings
The chorus of quietude
This frequency of unknown things
Do not fight with the sky
When she welcomes every season
And all those messages
The turbulent clouds bring

My spirit is not free
If yours cannot breathe
Let's allow love
And see what transpires
Of anarchy and alchemy

Naked
As winter's trees
Exposed and free
Having shed these dead leaves
The proof lies below you
The promise, above
Have you allowed yourself to breathe
Now that you do not have to carry
The landscape
Of what others choose to see
Just rest in your roots
The strong branches remain barren
Unapologetically

When the heart can breathe
The ghosts are free

I will watch
Until I get it right
I will wait
Just to be sure
Simmering in stillness
Until the soft walls of my heart
Remind me I am strong

Such space rests in the murky shadows
Removed from the demand
Of needing to see
Everything existing
Organically
And you-
Wide open to all ambiguity
I am watching
As you are waiting
Just to be relieved
Of the shield around your neck
So, I wonder
Where, dare you
Undress next

Let me love you
In fits and starts
The way summer rain cannot decide
Moody and mighty
My heart wants the whole of the sky
And you beside me
When the moon claims the night

If you lay down your weapons
It is no longer war
What surrenders to the earth
Nurtures peace, evermore

It is when I close my eyes
In that quiet meadow of sleep
That I can finally remember
All the somethings and nothings in our way
And here my heart
Knows how to listen
Weighted gently
Upon your chest
When my mind is finally quiet
Choosing your love
Feels effortless

What if we are all just flowers
Spreading our seeds
And establishing roots
Wherever we go
What if home
Is everywhere
You shed your tears
Magic waters
Helping you grow

I am a dreamer of undeniable things
Because I feel spirit
When the flowers bloom
And I do not weep
When they wither
For I welcome the beauty
Surrendering brings

Hold me gentle with your eyes
The way the moon
Graces the night sky
Never fear the dusky sides
What hides behind what is bright
There is nothing to resist
Waiting
 Within the arms of love's light

I will let the tide carry
The weight of what I see
My arms open wide
No longer am I a thief
Holding tightly to what is not mine
Hanging on
To these grips of time
I am sand
Collecting rocks
Washing ashore
Once the waves roll and rest
Where I wait in the night
To be revealed
Inspired
No longer bereft

I sat to watch the trees
A master class in how to bend
By way of what leaves
Haphazardly graceful
Barren and still
Beautiful in their unbecoming
Solid in their will

My soul is tired
But I am listening
To the pauses between breaths
Hope whispers
Stillness is the test
Truth resonates from deep within the bones
Aching with the currents
Strong like stones
So I will sit with resolve
Softening around the edges
Letting all the darkness that surrounds
Fall away from the ledges

Tell me about
This constellation of scars
So I know how to look
At your night sky
With wonder and awe
This evidence of truth
Let me bear witness
Just you and I
Together
Beneath the hold
Of the moon

Let me put my feet in the sand
Remember my wings
Lift off when I hear it calling
Stand firm
While I wait to see what clarity brings
Or watch as I become water
When I fall with grace
It is cleansing. Reminding
To not be of any one place
Where I belong is where I stand
Who knows when the elements will arise
Shape shifting me again

Next time you fall to pieces
And the ground begins to fill
Marvel at the fault lines
Let your seeds spill
Fertile ground
Knows no enemy
Where the rivers and the rocks coexist
At the banks the ground is still
For the waters are wise
Swelling with purpose
Flooding at will

This water you feel
Never remains
A shape ever-changing
Her solid form
Cannot be claimed
Like hope, unplanted
Love, unchained
This river ever flowing
Diffuses the debris
Which has muddied your radiance
And keeps the energy from glowing

This desperate ache
Has grown my heart
So that yours might bleed
And still, I believe
In love's grace
I choose giving
Trusting that our coming apart
Is but a joining together
Once we allow
All the corners and the walls
What our defenses build
To weather away and wither

If I let you go
Might I catch myself
Free or falling

Jennifer Goodine

The whole world is burning
Yet, these still waters
Call you home

There is nothing I want more
Then anything I could possibly own
Through its very existence
Speaks to the desire
I have yet to know
And right now
This moment is calling
As the sun whets the treetops
Her light is gracefully falling
Morning stretches amongst the sky
While I awaken
A reverent knowing
Alas, I have already arrived

I wait all year
For the leaves to die
For the beauty of the crimson sky
For permission to become
The strength to fly
I long for September
Her alchemy of demise
I covet autumn's rebel heart
The brilliant October
Unfolding in your eyes

Sovereignty
When I know I can flee
But choose to meet the moment
And let the moment wash over me
Not shielding the sun
Or seeking her shadows
Not racing toward the horizon
When it is the landscape that matters
It is a knowing unknown
Born only of trust
An allowing of the pouring rain
Never fearing what might rust

For every tempest
There is a dawn
An oceanic homecoming
Where your spirit is reborn
A clearing away
And a bringing forth
Towards your inner light compass
Pointing north

For the sake of my heart
I have decided
To unseal my eyes
Drink hope into my chest
Emancipate all cravings
Flow within the breath
Release my grip on time
Pinch myself alive
Slowly, with humility
Leave behind
All the many things
Which have imprisoned me in rigidity

STILLNESS

I will not die before I live
I want to see all the colors
And every season the sky has to give

Advice to my daughter:
If your heart is breaking
Allow the ache
Where it hurts
Is where it matters
And where it matters
Lies the work
And the work is your reward
Tiny blessings often look like mistakes
Stay curious
For these are gifts
Listen with love. Do not ignore

There have been years that grew me
Years that broke my back
Although, my heart never waivers
It remains intact
But this love we have curated
Through joy and shared plight
Has morphed before us
At least a hundred times
And no longer do I see that girl
So unsure and afraid of life
But I feel us together
Just beside chaos and wonder
And I realize
There is no other imaginable way
I would rather
Wait
War
Or wander

You see what you want to see

Through lonely eyes

But the heart knows

Love's truth

Even when it tries to hide

For you are never separate

From all that bleeds

Or breaks

Or buckles

In a time of need

Just listen closely

To that gentle song

Whispering in your ear

We are everything and everything is God

A reverent hand
Holds all hearts
To the divine

I want to be loved
Like the night cradles the moon
Content to let her shine

I've learned to love my scars
They whisper the stories
Of magic and madness
And send hope
To hungry hearts

Let me sit beside you
Midnight calls again
We'll hold hands
With our eyes closed
And in the peace
Remember
A love so simple
Shared hopes and fears
Between the best of friends

Two things can be certain
At the very same time
Have you never seen a rainbow
Grace the angry sky

Let your fortitude roar
From the well of your knowing
The depths of who you are
Sometimes opposition will win the war
But if you can only just pause
And arm yourself in stillness
You might discover liberation
Standing before a closed door

By all means move
If it allows you to be
Quiver your bones awake
So your tired mind might find ease
Let life reacquaint you
To the ecstasy
When you dance
Wandering within the words
Your heart longs to hear
And when no one is looking
Release your tears
Just let it all shake
Loosen the contents of your head
Tiny earthquakes
Wake
Both the sleeping and the dead

Home was never really a place
It is the people I love
The forest and her trees
Sea salted
Golden skin
Bared to breathe
Memories, like moments
Our solitude in sync
It's your hand in mine
This open road before us
Forsaking destination
And the wasted need to think

Jennifer Goodine

There are many ways
To learn about love
Leaving and loss
Sunshine and storms
Patience and solitude
Forgiveness, unarmed
Giving away
Allowing in
Sitting in the darkness
Quietly
Beside him

Leave alone
This space you seek to fill
Love will move the mountains
Grounded by your will

Respect is the language of love
Which whispers
I will see
What you cannot
Pain, like midnight
Blurs sight lines
I will hold your heart
Before my eyes
You will never have to worry
My heart doesn't mind

Home is where
My head finds your chest
Softening upon
Where your heart is cleft
Divinity sparks
As your hand
Finds my own
Silently content
Within the liminal spaces
Where love is grown

Practice the pivot
The posture of love

When the world is quiet
And you are still
Can you allow the spaces
Without a rush to fill
Every moment
Undetermined to be
Will you let it unfold
Should your eyes not see
Such curiosity
Simply waiting
For a heart and hands
Humbly anticipating

Jennifer Goodine

The wisdom of us

Never lies

It is silent

Ever- knowing

No matter the confusion

Swirling in your eyes

What weight grounds our hands

When the world feels too much

A promise, unbroken

Our love, a rush

Together walking

These foreign paths

Littered with stones and hope

Avowing the past with such respect

And the future bespoke

To love me
First find center
In a breath
A moment sacred
Undisturbed by its death
Careful steps in the night
Idiosyncrasy you allow
Unmoved to be right
Take my hand, unclaiming
Return to my curiosity
Never hesitating
Be a rock
And the ocean
Please remember
Love is our peace
Steady, in motion

Of land and water
I've loved you best
Entrenched to the earth
And the waves will attest
I do not waiver from my heart
Veins like grooves
So deep along
The ridges of time
Spirits of the wind
Your soul and mine
Brilliantly ablaze
Igniting what cannot be seen
Beneath the stories
Conjured deep within your dreams

There is always an opening
If you just search for what is bright
Nevertheless, an ending
If it only matters who is right
Just focus onward
Inside and up above
The path of happiness
We paint with possibility
Using all the shades and colors
From the edge
Of our prismatic love

Of wisdom and war
The truth that sets me free
Pieces of armor
No longer required
For this heart
Can deeply breathe
And these feelings
Like rainbows
Transiently shine
Finite as the fires
Awakening my mind
No bother or worry
I shall stand and burn
Transfixed by the embers
Simply allowing
Love's return

Gratitude

To all my teachers, all the souls who have shared both their light and their darkness with me, thank you for showing me the way.

To the dear friends, who were early readers, the supporters, my muse, thank you for giving my work a reason to breathe.

To Ryan and Marsha, who put in so much time and detail from behind the screen, thank you for pushing me through the technical parts that made me want to never complete this project. For seeing the path forward. For believing.

To my family, thank you for being. Especially Mom and Dad, who will forever exist in my heart. I hope you know. I hope you are proud.

About the Author

Jennifer Goodine is a yoga teacher and writer living in Connecticut with her two children and husband and her favorite four-legged friend, Roscoe. When she's not writing or teaching, you'll find her enjoying the natural world, walking or hiking, enjoying a good book, or finding a good reason to escape to the beach.

You can connect with Jennifer and practice yoga with her online at wisewarrioryoga.com and @jengoodinepoet on Instagram.

Photo Credit: Shannen L. Patnoad Photography

Thank you to my favorite girl in the whole of the world, Sophia Goodine, for sketching out my vision for the cover. For what I can only create with words, she can bring to life with art.

Coda

They are only words
Disparate like sand
Disappearing in solitude
Slipping through your hands
But if you hold their meaning
Close to your chest
Where warmth burgeons
From the crater loss has left
They fuse together
Like lonely stars
Conglomerating into something new
Make your own meaning
From what has washed over you
For like the river
Which tumbles the rocks
Or the vastness of the night sky
You have powers untouched
And to understand the secret message
Only you know why

Made in the USA
Middletown, DE
01 February 2023